UnAnxious

UNANXIOUS

An Hachette UK Company
www.hachette.co.uk

Vie Books, an imprint of Summersdale Publishers Ltd
Part of Octopus Publishing Group Limited
Carmelite House
50 Victoria Embankment
LONDON
EC4Y 0DZ
UK

www.summersdale.com

Printed and bound in China

ISBN: 978-1-78783-672-3

Substantial discounts on bulk quantities of Summersdale books are available to corporations, professional associations and other organizations. For details contact general enquiries: telephone: +44 (0) 1243 771107 or email: enquiries@summersdale.com.

DISCLAIMER
The author and the publisher cannot accept responsibility for any misuse or misunderstanding of any information contained herein, or any loss, damage or injury, be it health, financial or otherwise, suffered by any individual or group acting upon or relying on information contained herein. None of the views or suggestions in this book is intended to replace medical opinion from a doctor who is familiar with your particular circumstances. If you have concerns about your health, please seek professional advice.

UnAnxious

How to Manage
Your Worries,
Transform Your
Attitude and
**Feel More
Positive**
Every Day

Claire Chamberlain

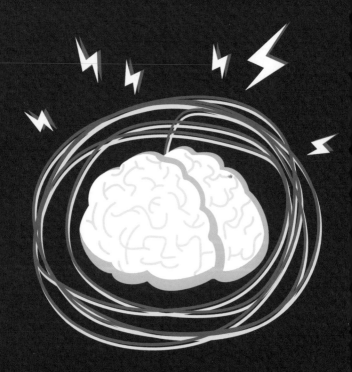

INTRODUCTION

Most of us know what anxiety feels like: worries spiralling around your brain or "butterflies" flapping in your stomach are common symptoms. And the truth, as uncomfortable as it may be, is that anxiety is a normal human emotion that we're all likely to experience from time to time. Problems arise only when these episodes become intense and commonplace, popping up in unnecessary situations on a daily basis, and making happiness and peace of mind seem impossible. Whatever the cause of your anxiety, it can create real pain, leaving you feeling isolated and alone.

This book is designed to help you understand where your anxiety comes from and why you're experiencing it, before offering a series of practical steps, inspiring ideas and uplifting affirmations to support and guide you. Read it from cover to cover, or dip into it whenever worry takes hold: it will help you to build a more resilient mentality and support you in caring for your mind, body and soul.

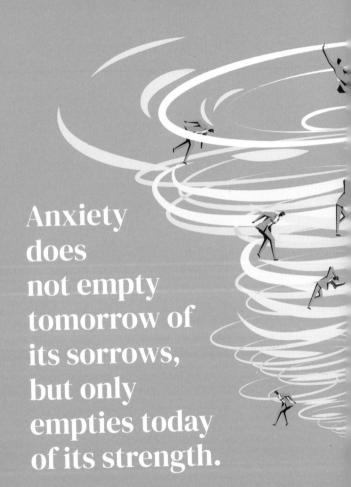

Anxiety
does
not empty
tomorrow of
its sorrows,
but only
empties today
of its strength.

Charles Spurgeon

What is anxiety?

Anxiety tends to be characterized by feelings of unease, worry or dread, often in relation to future or imagined events. While most people experience anxious thoughts from time to time, such as during periods of change or uncertainty, chronic anxiety (which means it persists over a long time) is a genuine mental health condition that can impact heavily on your life.

If you think you may be suffering from an anxiety disorder, know that you're not alone: the World Health Organization reports that these are the most common mental disorders worldwide, with one in 13 people suffering globally. There's no shame in experiencing anxiety, and this book will show you that there are things you can do to make life better.

WHAT'S "NORMAL" ANYWAY?

Sometimes, you might question whether you have a normal level of anxiety... but just what is "normal" when it comes to your mental health? As with lots of things in life, there is no black and white, only many shades of grey, and what seems manageable for one person may feel unbearable to another. Broadly speaking, though, if you occasionally experience mild to moderate anxiety levels in relation to a specific, upcoming event – such as a job interview – and if this sensation feels pretty much in proportion to the situation, it's likely you're experiencing "normal" anxiety, and it probably won't impact your life too much.

If, on the other hand, you feel worried a lot of the time, you constantly visualize worst-case scenarios, your anxiety feels out of proportion to situations, you struggle to sleep, or you've started avoiding certain places, events, friends or social gatherings because of your anxiety, then you may need a helping hand in learning to manage these feelings. It's OK, though... there are lots of ways you can start to help yourself.

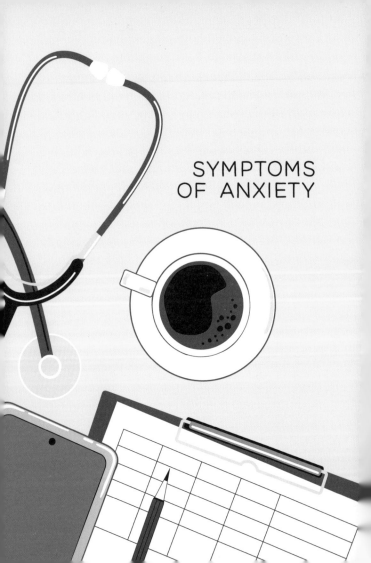

SYMPTOMS
OF ANXIETY

Anxiety can bring with it a range of symptoms, both mental and physical. The former might include excessive worrying, feelings of dissociation (such as feeling disconnected from your body), agitation, restlessness, stress, fatigue, irritability and insomnia. Physical symptoms can include muscle tension, a racing heart, "butterflies" in your stomach, nausea, headaches, dizziness and shallow breathing. Some physical symptoms, such as shortness of breath and even chest pain, can sometimes make you think that you are seriously ill.

Depending on the kind and intensity of the symptoms you're experiencing, you may be diagnosed by a medical professional with a specific anxiety disorder; some of the most common ones include generalized anxiety disorder (GAD), social anxiety disorder, panic disorder, phobias, obsessive compulsive disorder (OCD) and post-traumatic stress disorder (PTSD). These can sound scary, so we're going to look at some in a bit more detail over the following pages, before we explore things you can do to address and alleviate all types of anxiety.

OUR ANXIETY DOES NOT COME FROM THINKING ABOUT THE FUTURE, BUT FROM WANTING TO CONTROL IT.

Kahlil Gibran

Generalized anxiety disorder (GAD)

If you experience chronic anxiety relating to a wide range of situations and issues, you may be suffering from generalized anxiety disorder (GAD). This can see you feeling anxious most days, with uncontrollable worries bringing on symptoms such as restlessness, unease, irritability, a sense of dread and difficulty sleeping. GAD can feel all-consuming, but you're not the only one feeling this way: the NHS suggests 5 per cent of the UK population suffers from it, while in the US, data from National Comorbidity Survey Replication indicates that 5.7 per cent of American adults experience GAD at some point in their lives.

SOCIAL ANXIETY
DISORDER

Social anxiety is more than simply feeling shy; it's an overwhelming fear of social situations, which can have a huge impact on your life. It usually starts during the teenage years and, while some people grow out of it as they get older, many do not. Common symptoms of social anxiety include worrying about everyday activities, such as meeting new people, going to work, shopping or speaking on the phone; anxiety about eating in public; and fear of social situations and the thought of being observed. Physical symptoms include blushing, nausea and panic attacks. Sadly, social anxiety can also lead to feelings of loneliness and low self-esteem, if your fears cause you to become increasingly isolated. The good news, though, is there are lots of self-help techniques to help you overcome social anxiety disorder, as well as professional help, should you need it.

Panic disorder

Panic disorder is a form of anxiety that means you regularly experience panic attacks. These involve an abrupt onset of intense fear, usually lasting between 5 and 20 minutes; while you're in the grip of one, it can feel terrifying. During a panic attack, symptoms tend to build rapidly and can include shallow breathing, a racing heart, shaking, sweating, chest pain and the sense you're about to collapse. It's frightening, but focusing on slowing your breathing during an attack can help it ease.

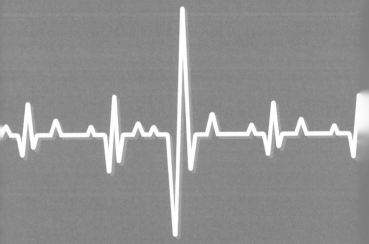

Obsessive compulsive disorder (OCD)

If you're caught in a cycle of recurring, obsessive thoughts that lead to repetitive compulsions, you may be suffering from OCD. The drive to perform compulsive behaviours is strong; while you may find they temporarily ease feelings of stress, ultimately these ritualistic actions can take over your life, interfering with daily activities and causing significant stress. Obsessions often have themes, such as a fear of dirt or needing everything in perfect order, with compulsions including washing, counting and needing to adhere to strict, self-imposed routines. Breaking the cycle can seem scary, but it is possible with professional help.

One of our greatest
freedoms is how we
react to things.

Charlie Mackesy

Post-traumatic stress disorder (PTSD)

Many people who go through or witness a traumatic event will need time to adjust. But if you experience intrusive memories (such as nightmares or flashbacks), negative changes in mood, or changes in physical or emotional reactions (such as insomnia or irritability), and these symptoms worsen over time or last for months (or even years), you may be experiencing PTSD. The intensity of symptoms may vary over time and can be triggered by sudden reminders (such as the sound of fireworks or a story on the news). Fear, anxiety and guilt are also common reactions to trauma. Don't be scared to turn to those you trust for support, but you should seek out professional expertise if you feel overwhelmed.

Body dysmorphic disorder (BDD)

Symptoms of BDD include comparing your appearance to other people's, worrying about specific areas of your body, feeling anxious about your "flaws" (which are often imagined or imperceptible to others), spending considerable time trying to hide such "flaws" with make-up or clothes, and either constantly checking mirrors or avoiding them altogether. BDD is not a sign of vanity. It is a serious and distressing mental health condition – one that affects both men and women. It's important to seek help – whether that's through learning to practise self-care and mindfulness techniques, joining support groups or therapy – because if left unchecked, BDD can lead to depression, eating disorders, self-harm or even suicidal thoughts.

DON'T BE PUSHED BY YOUR PROBLEMS. BE LED BY YOUR DREAMS.

Ralph Waldo Emerson

ECO-ANXIETY

Eco-anxiety can spring from feelings of uncertainty, helplessness and frustration in the face of climate change. It's a growing phenomenon, demonstrating that global warming is not just damaging the planet, but also our mental health. As well as the stress caused by witnessing climate change unfold, many people are also experiencing worries about the future, for both themselves and the next generations.

But what can be done about it? Self-help techniques and professional support in the form of CBT (see page 145) can be effective. But it's worth emphasizing that many scientists and psychologists believe eco-anxiety is actually a healthy response to this threat. In order to manage this anxiety so that it's not harmful to your mental well-being, it's important to acknowledge its validity, and then find ways of channelling the worry and stress into positive action. This might be by making changes to your personal behaviour, in order to live in a more environmentally friendly way, or by joining activist groups or support networks. The key is to lessen the anxiety by using it to fuel proactive, positive change.

WHY DO WE
FEEL ANXIOUS?

Whether you suffer from a specific anxiety disorder or not, you will likely know what anxiety feels like – that sense of unease or dread. But why do we feel anxious?

From an evolutionary perspective, the ability to experience anxiety serves to alert us to (and therefore protect us from) potential future threats. A precursor to fear's "fight, flight or freeze" response, anxiety acts as the alarm signalling that our attention is needed. Historically, anxiety may have alerted us to life-threatening events or situations.

Sometimes, modern-day anxiety can be helpful, too. It can focus our attention on an upcoming event that we need to prepare for, or motivate us to work hard for an exam or job interview. As we've learned, it's only when the anxiety becomes too intense or prolonged – and has no outlet – that it becomes harmful to our mental health.

Anxiety also often rears its head in situations where we feel a sense of helplessness: worrying about something over which we have no control means there's no positive outlet for our heightened focus, making us vulnerable to both the physical and mental symptoms of anxiety. The good news is that there are lots of practical steps you can take to help soothe your mind and calm the anxious voice in your head.

Anxiety and guilt

Feelings of guilt can both cause and be created by anxiety, and the intertwining nature of the two can make them a damaging combination. Of course, guilt can have benefits when it's appropriate: it can alert us to behaviour that is hurtful to others or ourselves, and it can be the trigger that sparks positive change. The problems come if the guilt is unnecessary (it's something we don't need to feel guilty about) or we hold on to it for too long. Accepting responsibility, understanding you're not perfect (no one is), taking action if necessary and then moving on can help you to manage guilt in a healthier way.

Modern living and stress

The pace of life has accelerated so rapidly in recent times that many of us experience daily stress and anxiety in relation to modernity. No longer led by our natural rhythms and body clock, we tend to work longer hours, have increased screen time, move less and spend fewer hours outside in the natural world – all of which can weigh heavily on both our minds and bodies. Learning to slow down or pause, even for a moment, can help to counteract this frenetic pace of life. Some of the tips later on in this book offer actionable ways of easing your foot off life's accelerator.

CAN YOU REALLY
"HAVE IT ALL"?

The pressure to be all things to all people can be a source of anxiety and stress for many. Expectations (often placed on us by ourselves) to be a good parent, exemplary employee, supportive partner, great friend or loving child can leave us feeling stretched too thin, sometimes with nothing left to give to ourselves at the end of each day.

Or course, having a great career, loving family and good social life is brilliant, and it's something many of us aspire to. But it will only feel fulfilling if we're not chasing these things at the detriment of our own mental health. Burning the candle at both ends can leave us feeling tired, stressed and even guilty that we can only dedicate fractions of our lives to certain roles. The good news here is that you don't (and shouldn't) have to do everything by yourself. Giving yourself some headspace, whether that's by delegating work projects, or enlisting additional support from a partner or family member, will give you a little more breathing room – valuable me-time that allows you to work on restoring your own mental balance.

The problem with perfection

Perfectionism can sound like a positive trait. After all, striving for perfection proves you're hard-working, driven and ambitious, right? The problem is that perfection is unattainable and the desire to reach this lofty height can quickly become an all-consuming obsession. What's more, the fear of falling short often creates a sense of paralysis; knowing you might not be perfect means you become too scared to even try. If you're a perfectionist, try letting go of any unrealistic expectations you set yourself. The truth is that being "good enough" really is good enough.

Perfectionism is just
fear in fancy shoes
and a mink coat.

Elizabeth Gilbert

FEAR OF MISSING OUT

If you frequently find yourself worrying that others are having rewarding, fulfilling experiences while you're not, you may be suffering from fear of missing out (FOMO). The anxiety caused by FOMO is very real, and it can lead to you constantly messaging your contacts or scrolling through social media sites in an attempt to seek out more and more connections. It can see you interrupting one online chat to start another, and have you checking your phone while in the company of friends and family – or even while at work – to make sure you don't "miss out". Of

course, the reality is that FOMO can mean pushing people close to you away, as you get sucked into the unreality of the online world. If you're beginning to feel that your FOMO is damaging your mental health, try talking to someone you trust about how social media is making you feel. Perhaps schedule in some screen-free moments each day – even just half an hour – and, instead of scrolling, spend the time doing something that makes you feel happy, such as reading, drawing or yoga. In short, try swapping FOMO for JOMO (the "joy of missing out").

How do you compare?

As well as FOMO, social media opens up numerous opportunities for us to compare ourselves to our peers – often unfavourably. These constant comparisons can leave us feeling anxious that we aren't as successful/pretty/slim/adventurous as others, and they do little for our mental health. Next time you find yourself scrolling through social media, keep in mind that people generally only share the best bits of their lives, where they're looking and feeling great, or doing something exciting or accomplished. Nobody's real life looks like this, even if it appears that way. Stop comparing your everyday moments to a stranger's highlights reel.

Right here, right now, you are enough

RELATIONSHIP
ANXIETY

Anxiety within a relationship can have a big impact on your whole life, and it can arise for a wide range of reasons. Whether you're dealing with issues of trust, respect or self-worth, the management of your anxiety will very much depend on its cause. If you have worries relating to trust, for example, is this due to a previous betrayal or is your current partner behaving in a way that creates conflict and anxiety? Is it something you need to work on individually or might you benefit from couples therapy to help you deal with a specific problem? Take time to decide the best way forward, and don't be pressured by your partner into a decision you aren't comfortable with. With support and understanding, you can navigate this anxiety together, while strengthening your bond. If your partner is reluctant to listen to you, or is constantly dismissive of your fears or feelings, it's OK to question whether it's time to walk away. As scary as this can seem, sometimes it's the right decision.

Anxiety and loneliness

Sadly, loneliness is often intrinsically linked with feelings of anxiety, although it's frequently hard to distinguish between the cause and the effect. On the one hand, loneliness can trigger anxious thoughts, and feeling like you don't have a support network to hand can be detrimental to your mental health. On the other hand, your anxiety may make you withdraw from those around you, leading to a greater sense of isolation. If you're feeling lonely, a simple first step could be to message someone you trust, as that could spark a conversation and sense of connection. Or you might want to reframe being on your own as a form of valuable solitude.

A note on bereavement

The loss of a loved one is always painful. Please remember: there is no right or wrong way to grieve – it's a personal experience, unique to you. If you suffer from mental health issues, such as anxiety, be aware that bereavement can be a powerful trigger, so don't be afraid to ask for help if you're struggling. Try to allow yourself to feel your emotions, however difficult it can be, rather than bottling your grief up. Talking to others and sharing memories of the person who has died can be cathartic.

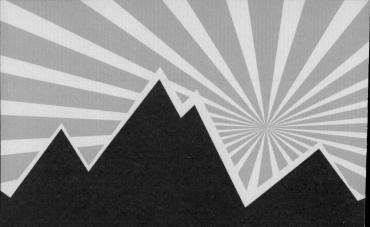

Managing your mental health: the first steps

Living with anxiety is a painful experience. Whether you've struggled with it for days or years, its presence can be debilitating, robbing you of your happiness and peace of mind. While it can leave you feeling helpless, it's important to accept that you are not: acknowledging the problem – and resolving to do something about it – is an incredibly brave and important first step. Even doing something as seemingly small as flicking through the pages of this book is powerful and proactive: it's a sign you're not willing to give up on yourself. Hang in there: things can (and will) get better.

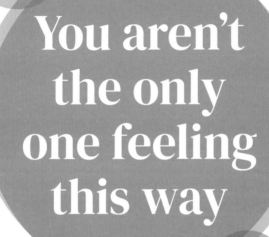

You aren't the only one feeling this way

CHANGING
YOUR
RELATIONSHIP
WITH
ANXIETY

Until now, you might have viewed your anxiety as an enemy: an unwanted presence that has to be defeated and driven out. But perceiving it in this way can lead to additional stress – an added layer of pressure on top of the anxiety you're already trying to cope with. What's more, positioning your anxiety as the enemy leaves scope for failure: if you don't beat it, it has "won" and you've "lost". This attitude can lead to feelings of despair and even trigger the onset of depression. But it doesn't have to be this way.

As we've already explored, anxiety is your body's way of trying to protect you in the face of danger: it's a precursor to the "fight, flight or freeze" response, warning you that something may threaten your existence. It's therefore impossible to rid yourself of anxiety altogether – in fact, doing so might even be detrimental to your welfare. The key is to start managing your anxiety when it arises in everyday, non-life-threatening situations – to be able to watch it, acknowledge it and then move your thoughts away from it, so that it dissipates. Changing your relationship with anxiety in this way, by removing the battle, can have a profound effect on your state of mind. It's a subtle but profound shift in consciousness.

YOU DESERVE
TO BE HAPPY

When you're feeling happy, calm and positive, it's easy to treat yourself with love and kindness. But when you're struggling with feelings of anxiety, being kind to yourself can prove far more difficult. Perhaps you don't think you deserve happiness. But feeling undeserving in this way can create unconscious resistance to positive change, which means that, however much you tell yourself you want to move beyond your anxiety, you may inadvertently undermine your own efforts.

As difficult as it can seem, in order to move forward and make progress, you will need to accept – and truly believe – that you deserve happiness, no matter what has happened in your past. It's always OK to look after yourself, and you are always deserving of love and happiness.

Give yourself a break

An important step toward overcoming anxiety and improving your mental health is to become more accepting of yourself. Yes, you have weaknesses, but we all do, so try to give yourself a break. You're human, after all. Instead of focusing on everything you struggle with, start to acknowledge your strengths; rather than constantly striving to keep up, let yourself rest. By viewing yourself through a more compassionate lens, and by slowing down a little, you will make space in your life for positive, empowering change.

You can't pour from an empty cup

NOTICE YOUR
TRIGGERS

A "trigger" is a stressful situation, event or occurrence that sets off your anxiety. Your triggers may be unique to you, although there are lots of common ones that resonate with many people. Some might be obvious, such as an upcoming interview or exam, while others are less so. Perhaps you're not yet aware of what your triggers are – or maybe you're aware of some of them, but not others.

If you notice the physical symptoms of anxiety rising up within you, chances are something in that moment has triggered you. To gain a better understanding of your anxiety and how to control it, identifying your triggers is a great place to start. Next time you begin to feel anxious, take note of what has happened in the moments immediately preceding that feeling. What thoughts flitted through your head? Where were you? What were you doing? What had you eaten or drunk? Sometimes the trigger can be physiological, such as the effects of the caffeine in your morning cup of coffee. Ultimately, an awareness of your triggers can help you to manage your anxiety, giving you the chance to address the causes head-on.

MAPPING PATTERNS

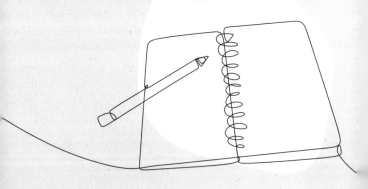

To help you gain a better understanding of your triggers, as well as the pattern of your anxiety, it can be a good idea to chart your emotions in a diary. By consistently noting down everything relevant – including thoughts, encounters, journeys and tasks – you can start to build a comprehensive picture of the nature of your anxiety, allowing you to notice patterns. For example, you might become aware that your anxiety is related to meetings with a particular person, that it arises at a particular time of day or that it is linked to hormonal changes in your body.

You don't have to write things down in a specific way or in a fancy journal – a notebook will do. Simply jot down the date, events, occurrences, thoughts and emotions – whatever feels relevant. It may take a while to notice a pattern, so give yourself time and try to be consistent, aiming to jot things down for six to eight weeks.

You may also find that the simple act of writing down your thoughts and feelings is cathartic in itself and that putting your worries down on paper removes their power.

STRENGTHEN
YOUR MINDSET

Anxiety can make you feel small. Sometimes it can seem bigger than you – huge enough to engulf you – but remember: you are bigger than it is, always. Facing up to anxiety takes guts, but you are brave enough. There isn't a quick fix, so you will need to harness your resilience. It's OK to fail sometimes. It's also normal to feel like you're making progress for a few days, before encountering a setback and thinking that you're back at square one again. You're not; each time you try – even if you don't get the results you're aiming for – you are learning and accumulating vital information, and training your brain in a different way. So approach the challenge of overcoming your anxiety with compassionate boldness: yes, it's important to be gentle with yourself, but always believe that you are strong enough... and never give up hope.

Challenge negative thought patterns

It's easy to fall into the trap of believing everything you think. But thoughts are just thoughts. I'm not good enough or I won't be able to cope are examples of thoughts that are probably masquerading as facts in your mind, but they are negative, unhelpful and untrue. Next time you notice yourself getting sucked into a negative thought, stop for a moment (you can literally think the word "stop" to cut it off). Then ask yourself: is this true? Really challenging these negative thoughts can change the way you view yourself – and the world around you.

The greatest weapon
against stress is our
ability to choose one
thought over another.

William James

You're amazing! Never forget it.

Stop wondering, "What if…"

Anxiety is often rooted in the fear of possible or imagined future outcomes. Asking yourself: "What if…?" tends to lead to catastrophic thinking, where you play out worst-case scenarios on a loop in your mind. As soon as you find yourself worrying "What if…?", catch yourself and draw your attention to your current surroundings. Are you safe right now? Notice something you can see, then something you can hear. Grounding yourself in the present moment in this way, rather than skipping ahead to negative possibilities, can help to keep anxiety at bay. And those future what-ifs. They probably won't happen.

Try not to dwell

While anxiety is often felt in relation to a future possibility, it's also common to experience it in relation to the past. Do any of the following sound familiar: I wish I hadn't said that; I feel so embarrassed about that; was I funny/kind/brave enough? The truth is, it's easy to look back over past encounters and come up with different (normally better) outcomes in your head – that's the beauty of hindsight, as well as its curse. Dwelling on the past is futile: it's already happened and there's nothing you can do to change it. Instead, vow to stop ruminating and start focusing on the present moment. What positive step can you take today?

Worry often gives a small thing a big shadow.

Swedish proverb

SEPARATE WHAT YOU
CAN CONTROL FROM
WHAT YOU CAN'T

Try writing a list of all the things that contribute toward your anxiety. You might include moments from your past that you still fret over, upcoming events, encounters with particular people, or situations that you find threatening or scary. You may find yourself jotting down day-to-day experiences that affect only you, as well as far-reaching global issues. The act of writing down your anxieties can have a calming effect, as seeing them in black and white, instead of floating freely around your mind, can make them appear more manageable.

Next, draw a line through everything that's out of your control. These will likely be things that have already happened, and therefore you can't change, or situations where other people are involved. Now take a look at your list. Are there actions you can take that will have a positive impact on the remaining worries? Global issues can seem so huge you may think you can't make a difference, but look more closely: could you join an activist group, donate to a cause or read up on an issue to educate yourself more fully? Taking positive, tangible action can help to ease anxiety.

Close the loop

A long mental to-do list can cause (or add to) feelings of anxiety. Next time a task pops into your head – something that's maybe been nagging away at you for a while now – either act on it straightaway or set yourself a reminder to deal with it at a later date. Examples include making a medical appointment, calling a family member or paying a particular bill. By doing it or diarizing it, you will close the open "loop" (recurring thought) in your head, giving yourself a bit more breathing space.

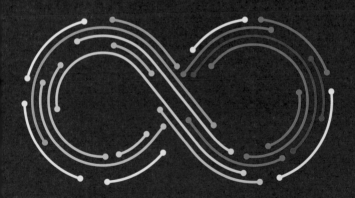

LET GO OF
THE PAST

FOCUS ON
NOW

Repeat a mantra

A mantra is a simple saying or slogan that you can repeat to yourself daily. Mantras are useful, as they can help to rewire your thoughts and create positive feelings or intentions. Many people find them life-changing. To ensure it's as transformative as possible, choose something that's easy to remember and that means something to you, as you embark on your journey to a calmer state of mind. "This too shall pass" or "I am strong, worthy and beautiful" are powerful examples.

If you don't like
something, change it.
If you can't change it,
change your attitude.

Maya Angelou

SOFTEN YOUR
LANGUAGE

Semantics is important, and the language you use when you speak to yourself can have a big impact on your mental health. Just think about the difference between telling yourself you "should" do something and telling yourself you "could" do something. "Should" implies you have to do it, even if you don't want to. There is also an element of pressure, which can add a layer of stress to your thinking. "Could", on the other hand, implies there's a choice.

Phrases such as "I have to..." and "I always..." can have the same stress-inducing effect as "should". Changing your language by replacing these common words and phrases with softer alternatives, such as "I might..." and "I sometimes..." can help to relieve some of the pressure you might be inadvertently placing on yourself.

Question your inner self-critic

Do you ever find yourself assuming that others think the worst of you? "They think I'm boring" or "They'd rather be talking to someone else" are thoughts that feed anxiety, making you feel isolated and alone, even when in the company of others. But here's the thing: these thoughts don't belong to other people – they come from your own inner critic. The truth is, you have no idea what someone else thinks of you, because you can't see inside their head. In reality, they probably view you more kindly than you sometimes view yourself.

Be kind to yourself today

TRY MENTAL NOTING

If you often find yourself lost in a cycle of anxious thoughts, you could try this "mental noting" technique. Next time you realize that your mind has wandered off from whatever it is you happen to be doing, simply "note" what type of thought or feeling has distracted you, and then bring your attention back to what you are doing in the present moment. For example, you might be cooking dinner, but suddenly find yourself lost in a complex

"What if...?" worry about something going wrong in a meeting the next day. As soon as you realize that your attention has wandered away from the activity of cooking, gently interrupt the cycle by thinking, "This is anxiety" (thereby making a mental note), before drawing your attention back to the meal you're preparing.

Mental noting in this way shouldn't be loud or judgemental; it's meant to sound more like a soft whisper in your ear, nudging you back to the present moment. At first, you may find you're lost in anxious thoughts for a long while before noticing and mentally noting them, but the more you practise this technique, the quicker you will find yourself being able to move on in your present-moment awareness.

Believe in yourself

Forgive yourself
(and others)

Berating yourself for past mistakes, or holding grudges against others, is a sure-fire way to disrupt your peace of mind, and can see you tying your mind up in knots of pain and angst. You can begin unravelling these painful knots by gently forgiving yourself – and forgiving those around you. We are all human and we all make mistakes. Don't hold onto the past. Instead, learn from your experiences and embrace this fresh new moment. Say the words aloud if that helps you to let go of your anxious anger.

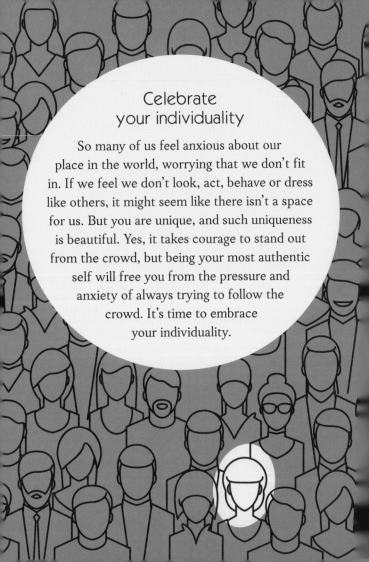

Celebrate your individuality

So many of us feel anxious about our place in the world, worrying that we don't fit in. If we feel we don't look, act, behave or dress like others, it might seem like there isn't a space for us. But you are unique, and such uniqueness is beautiful. Yes, it takes courage to stand out from the crowd, but being your most authentic self will free you from the pressure and anxiety of always trying to follow the crowd. It's time to embrace your individuality.

You bring something unique to the world

You probably wouldn't worry about what people think of you if you could know how seldom they do!

Olin Miller

Enlist a support network

Too many people suffer from anxiety or another mental health condition in silence. But sharing your pain with someone you trust can be cathartic, and sometimes just the act of talking about your anxiety can help to lessen the grip it has on you. Feeling understood is important, so try opening up to a close friend or family member. You might be surprised at how much they want to offer reassurance and support.

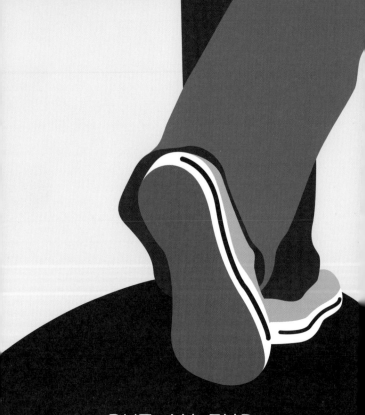

PUT AN END
TO DAMAGING
RELATIONSHIPS

Just as it's important to find people you can lean on in times of anxiety or mental distress, it's also crucial to distance yourself from those who contribute to your pain. Take a closer look at the relationships in your life – everything from romantic partnerships and friendships to wider acquaintances, as well as people you might not know personally but with whom you interact online. Do any make you feel uncomfortable, sparking uneasy emotions or feelings of anxiety? Is this something you feel you could work through or is it time to walk away? If a relationship is damaging to your mental health, removing yourself from the equation can sometimes be the healthiest option.

The importance of self-care

Anxiety often arises if you neglect your own physical and mental needs. If you regularly feel burned out at the end of each day, or that the pressures and strains of everyday life are leaving you no time to unwind and recharge, it's time to introduce a little self-care into your daily routine. Far from being selfish, taking time out to look after your own physical, mental, emotional and spiritual well-being is an essential practice.

SELF-CARE MEANS GIVING YOURSELF PERMISSION TO PAUSE.

Cecilia Tran

SEEK THE JOY IN EVERYDAY MOMENTS

Live more mindfully

Mindfulness is something of a buzzword these days. But how can you put it into practice – and how can it help to alleviate anxiety? Put simply, living mindfully means focusing your full attention on the present moment, exactly as it is, without judgement. This type of conscious awareness means that there is no room to ruminate on the past or worry about the future. Try concentrating on the rhythm of your breath, the feel of your feet on the floor and the ambience of your current surroundings – you'll find that anxiety won't be able to take hold.

Can you ever really "stop thinking"?

There are lots of misconceptions about mindfulness, one of the main ones being that it's a tool to stop thinking. But this is not the case – in fact, it's very difficult to stop thinking, as our thoughts help us to process the world around us. Rather than a way of getting rid of thoughts, mindfulness is the art of drawing our conscious attention to the here and now. You may find that worries (or those pesky what-ifs) sneak back into your mind. That's completely normal – don't beat yourself up about it, but as soon as you notice it happening, simply draw your attention back to the present moment.

INHALE DEEPLY.
EXHALE SLOWLY.
REPEAT.

IF YOU WANT TO CONQUER THE ANXIETY OF LIFE, LIVE IN THE MOMENT, LIVE IN THE BREATH.

Amit Ray

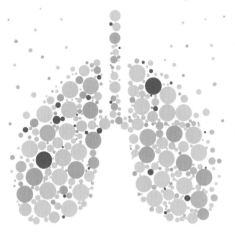

Breathe deeply

Gently slowing and lengthening your breath is a centuries-old practice to help lessen feelings of stress and anxiety, and it's one of the simplest forms of self-care. Breathing in this way engages your parasympathetic nervous system, which is responsible for feelings of relaxation and calm, and interrupts the sympathetic nervous system, which has been giving you those "fight, flight or freeze" responses. Take time out each day to notice your breathing – does it seem easy and relaxed, or short and shallow? Then consciously lengthen and slow your breath for a moment, to help melt away tension.

NOURISH YOUR BODY

In times of mental crisis, it can be easy to reach for sugary or high-salt comfort foods, such as chocolate or crisps, to get an immediate pick-me-up and keep battling on. Or perhaps anxiety makes you lose your appetite, meaning you don't adequately fuel yourself at all. However, if you don't nourish your body properly, you won't just suffer physically, but mentally too. Chocolate, crisps and biscuits all feel good in the short term, but there comes an inevitable crash as your blood sugar levels plummet, leaving you feeling anxious and irritable again.

Show yourself some love by eating wholesome, delicious foods. Make time to cook from scratch – search recipe books for meals that spark joy and happiness. Perhaps that's a colourful bowl of flavoursome curry, a hearty stew or a rainbow Buddha bowl. Opt for healthy snacks between meals that will help to keep your energy levels constant – avocado or peanut butter on wholemeal toast, a smoothie, or a simple banana are all great choices.

Drink more water

Even mild dehydration can impact your mood and emotional state, making you feel sluggish or dizzy, and it can even trigger anxiety. It's recommended that we drink between six and eight glasses of water a day (check your pee to see whether you're drinking enough – it should be a pale straw colour). Maintaining hydration throughout the day is an easy act of self-care – if you struggle to remember to refill your glass regularly, set an alarm or reminder on your phone. Your body and mind will thank you.

It's not selfish to love
yourself, take care of yourself
and make your happiness
a priority. It's necessary.

Mandy Hale

YOU ARE
STRONGER
THAN YOU
REALIZE

Limit your alcohol intake

If you find yourself turning to alcohol when feeling stressed or low, you're certainly not the only one. However, while those first few sips can invoke feelings of relaxation and release, this is often short-lived. In the long term, alcohol is likely to increase feelings of anxiety, agitation and worry, with additional negative consequences including disturbed sleep and fatigue – both of which contribute to poor overall health. Avoiding or limiting alcohol could see you feeling healthier, happier, less anxious and better able to deal with the challenges of everyday life.

Curl up with a book

If you find yourself caught in a cycle of anxious thoughts, try curling up on the sofa with a book. Rather than risk getting bogged down in a story that isn't to your liking, opt for something in your favourite genre or by a familiar author – maybe reread an old classic. Researchers have found that getting lost in the pages of an absorbing book can help to feel less stressed, as the act of reading offers a healthy escape from everyday life – something that many of us already know to be true.

What makes your soul happy?

Do more of that.

The present moment is filled
with joy and happiness. If you
are attentive, you will see it.

Thích Nhất Hạnh

Embrace your creativity

As humans, we are innately creative beings. There is so much joy to be found in the act of crafting something new; what's more, it can also be wholly cathartic and soothing for the mind. Writing, sketching, painting, sculpting and even doodling can all spark happiness, as well as helping to release pent-up tension or frustration. Don't worry about the end result (this can add to anxiety rather than ease it); the self-care and satisfaction lie simply in the act of creation.

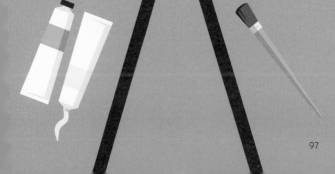

CONNECT WITH NATURE

Spending time outside in the natural world is proven to help alleviate anxiety – studies show that those who spend more time surrounded by nature experience improvements in mood, self-esteem and confidence, as well as physical health.

Making time to connect with Mother Nature daily – whether you have five minutes or five hours to spare – is a wonderful way of boosting your mental health. If you only have a short amount of time, try walking barefoot on the grass, taking your lunch break outdoors in a local park or stopping for a moment to listen to the birds singing. If you have more time, why

not give shinrin-yoku a go? The practice, which translates as "forest-bathing", involves immersing yourself in the sights, sounds and scents of a forest or woodland environment, by really slowing down and absorbing the calming surroundings.

Other ideas include sitting on a shoreline and listening to the waves, camping under the night sky or growing your own vegetables. No outside space? No problem! According to the UK's Royal Horticultural Society, numerous scientific studies have found that caring for houseplants improves psychological well-being.

Be still, even for a moment

Often, we get so caught up in our daily lives, rushing from one activity to the next, that we forget there is a quietness that resides within us, which we can access any time we wish to feel grounded. Try consciously pausing, just for a moment, a few times each day, to dissipate your feelings of stress and anxiety. Stop what you're focusing on, gently close your eyes and follow your breath for a count of ten. Simple, but effective.

Within you, there is a
stillness and a sanctuary
to which you can retreat at
any time and be yourself.

Hermann Hesse

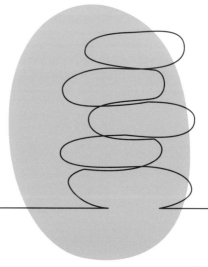

BOOST
YOUR FITNESS

Exercise is proven to boost not just your physical fitness, but also your mental health. As well as reducing anxiety, it increases feelings of well-being, and improves self-esteem and confidence (that'll be because of the endorphins – the happy hormones – that flood your body after a workout). What's more, as you start to exercise regularly, you begin to realize you're capable of more than you ever imagined, and this sense of possibility and potential can cross over to all areas of your life. Whatever fitness pursuit you love, be it jogging, cycling or Zumba, it's time to get moving!

Take a
digital detox

Have you ever said
to yourself you'll
have a "quick" scroll
through social media,
only to be left wondering
where those few hours went?
These sites can often fuel feelings of low self-
worth and, unfortunately, they are addictive. If
you've realized social media is doing you more
harm than good, a digital detox can help to break
this damaging cycle. Vow to spend a full day, or
even just an hour each day, away from your phone
(removing the temptation by placing it out of sight
will help) and instead invest in some quality self-
care and reflection.

You have come so far...

keep going!

Turn to meditation

Meditation is simply focused attention, for example on your breath, without judgement. Studies show that its positive benefits include reducing stress, lowering blood pressure and easing anxiety – simply put, it's a powerful yet simple tool to improve your well-being. To get started, find a quiet place where you won't be disturbed, gently close your eyes, and draw your attention to the rise and fall of your breath. If thoughts arise, acknowledge them without judgement, and then continue. Guided meditations are a wonderful entry point: there are lots of apps available to help you get started.

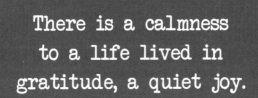

There is a calmness
to a life lived in
gratitude, a quiet joy.

Ralph H. Blum

Cultivate a positive outlook

When you're feeling low or anxious, there's
nothing more infuriating than someone telling
you to look on the bright side. It's important to
acknowledge the anxiety you are experiencing
and that your feelings are always valid. But
even when you're feeling anxious, naming one
positive thing in your life is a good way to start
cultivating a habit of positivity and optimism.
Acknowledging the good in your life, while
also accepting those painful moments, can
help you to hang in there. There is always a
glimmer of light, even in moments of darkness.

Write a list of your best qualities

While most of us could probably reel off a list of negatives about ourselves without a second thought, we are always far more reticent about our best qualities. But far from being a boastful exercise, recognizing and celebrating our unique attributes, as well as the skills we can offer the world, is an empowering act. Sit down with a notebook and spend a little time listing all your good qualities – perhaps you're a great cook, artist, parent or listener. Maybe you give the best hugs or always stand up for what you believe in. You're amazing – it's time you started believing it.

Let your positivity shine

Seek out beauty in everyday things

When you're caught in a spiral of anxiety, it's hard to appreciate your surroundings. But consciously seeking out and expressing gratitude for glimpses of beauty and joy in the world around you is a mindful act that can help to ground you positively in the here and now. Think there's nothing beautiful about your current situation? Start looking more closely: is that weed growing through the crack in the concrete covered in tiny flowers? How does the warmth of your morning tea make you feel? Does your time in the shower awaken your senses? It's all there, if you open your mind to it.

Be proactive

Accepting a problem, rather than burying your head in the sand, is important. Try breaking down large, overwhelming issues into smaller, more manageable chunks. For example, if financial worries are contributing to your anxiety, start tackling them straightaway – seek professional advice or start by paying off a single bill. Remember: taking even just one small step is far more productive and positive than trying to pretend nothing is wrong.

Declutter a room
(or even just a drawer)

A little mess and disorder in your home may seem unconnected to the anxiety you're feeling, but being constantly confronted with cluttered surfaces and cramped cupboards is commonly associated with stress. Try setting aside half an hour (or even just ten minutes) and commit to clearing out a drawer or two. Getting rid of material possessions that no longer serve you is cathartic and may serve to clear your mind, as well as your living space. Donating your unwanted items to charities or good causes doubles the benefits.

TUNE INTO YOUR SENSES

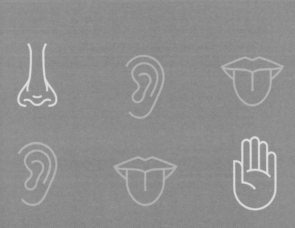

Next time you notice yourself getting caught in a spiral of anxious thoughts, try focusing all of your attention onto each of your senses in turn. This simple technique doesn't need to take long but is an effective way of grounding yourself in the present moment, exactly as it is, in a similar way to focusing on your breath.

First, tune into what you can see. You don't have to name objects; simply notice them, paying attention to colours, texture, light and shade. Next, focus on things you can hear. At first, this might be simply the sound of your own breath, but zone further out – what can you hear in the distance? Move through touch, smell and taste, giving each sense your full attention in the moment.

Be more wabi sabi

Life is not perfect, nor will it ever be. But you know what? That can be OK. The Japanese culture of wabi sabi encourages us to focus on the beauty of imperfection, to peacefully accept change and flux, and to acknowledge life exactly as it is. This allows us to notice the joy and beauty in everyday things, rather than dwelling on negatives or wishing that circumstances were different. Next time you feel anxiety rising, accept that feelings and emotions come and go, and embrace the beauty of the moment, grey skies and all.

Failure is a great teacher and,
if you are open to it, every
mistake has a lesson to offer.

Oprah Winfrey

CHECK UP ON OTHERS

Anxiety is an emotion that can lead to you centring your thoughts on yourself, so that you only notice negativity and fear in your own world. This is likely to make life feel quite claustrophobic, as well as giving you the impression that you have it worse than other people. To counter this, actively spend some time checking in with friends, family members or vulnerable people in your community, such as elderly neighbours. How are they doing, really? Could someone you know use a listening ear, a helping hand or even a shoulder to cry on? Being there for someone else who needs support is not only an important act of kindness, but it also widens your frame of reference, helping you to see there's more going on in the world than your own anxieties. If you spend a little time helping out – even though you're going through your own struggles – you can make a positive difference.

I'VE BEEN
SEARCHING
FOR WAYS TO
HEAL MYSELF,
AND I'VE FOUND THAT
KINDNESS
IS THE BEST WAY.

Lady Gaga

Perform random acts of kindness

You don't have to embark on huge performative gestures to demonstrate how much you care about others. Simple acts, such as holding a door open for someone, smiling at a stranger or sending a card to a friend, can brighten a person's day. And what's more, it can make you feel brighter, happier and more at peace, too.

PRACTISE GRATITUDE

Countless studies show the benefits of gratitude when it comes to both our physical and mental health. In fact, gratitude has been shown to help release toxic emotions, improve sleep quality, reduce stress, neutralize feelings of anxiety and depression, and even lessen the perception of physical pain. Researchers have found that expressing gratitude for what we have, as well as showing our appreciation of others, actually changes neural structures and pathways in the brain, making us feel happier and more content. If you'd like to start cultivating more gratitude in your life, you could begin by keeping a gratitude journal, in which you note down and reflect daily on all the good things in your life. Or you could start filling a gratitude jar: find a container and, each day, write down on a small piece of paper something you've felt grateful for; then fold it up and pop it inside. After a month, six months or even a year, you'll have a jar full of positivity that you can look back on to remind yourself of all the good in your life.

Book a massage

Massage therapy has been shown to provide relief from anxiety and stress by easing physical tension, aiding relaxation and promoting overall well-being. The hands-on physical contact can also be incredibly grounding, drawing your attention out of the mind and into the body. Booking an appointment with a registered practitioner is a great idea, but if this isn't an option for you, asking for a massage from a loved one or performing self-massage – on your shoulders, hands or feet – is also beneficial. Focus on the feel of your muscles being gently manipulated and visualize all your stress melting away.

you matter

MORE THAN

YOU KNOW

Treat yourself

Anxiety, stress and fear can all make you feel unworthy and undeserving, when in fact you are as worthy and deserving of joy and happiness as everyone else. So show yourself some love and TLC by treating yourself to something that will make you happy. It doesn't have to be a material present (although it can be, if you wish): a nap, a warm shower, time alone to read, a gentle walk or a hot cup of tea can all be wonderful gifts you give yourself and can remind you of how precious your mental health is.

Try some calming yoga poses

Yoga has long been used to help ease anxiety and calm the mind, and research supports its benefits. Even engaging in just one or two asanas (poses) each day, coupled with pranayama (controlling your breath), can positively impact your well-being. Asanas such as downward-facing dog, forward fold, cat and cow, tree, and child's pose can all invoke feelings of deep relaxation. If you sense your mind wandering and your thoughts scattering, accept and release them, before drawing your mind back to your practice.

Never give up on yourself

Wash away tension

When feeling anxious, it's common to hold tension in your body, particularly around your jaw and shoulders. Consciously drawing your attention to these areas and dropping this tension, by relaxing your shoulders back and down, and unclenching your jaw, can be helpful in releasing anxiety. Why not go a step further and wash away physical tension in a soothing warm bath? Adding a scoop of Epsom salts to the water can help to ease aching muscles – or use your favourite body wash and let the aroma relax your senses.

Talk to yourself
like you would to
someone you love.

Brené Brown

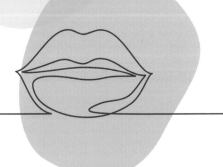

YOUR RESILIENCE IS INSPIRING

SET YOURSELF UP FOR BETTER SLEEP

Sleep is a vital physiological process that repairs your body and restores good mental function. Yet, sadly, anxiety and a good night's sleep don't often go hand in hand. Your body's "fight, flight or freeze" mode isn't conducive to drifting off peacefully at night. And the more you struggle to sleep, the worse your anxiety can become, trapping you in a vicious cycle.

If you find that sleep is elusive, good bedtime habits become even more important, but taking the pressure off yourself is also key. Try adopting a relaxing, restful evening routine, placing emphasis

on the pleasure of taking
care of yourself rather
than the end result.

Avoid caffeine from midday
and resist the temptation to
stare at screens in the two
hours before bedtime,
as the blue light they
emit messes with your
levels of sleep-inducing
melatonin. Try a warm,
relaxing bath or shower
before bed – the heat will
relax your muscles, while
the subsequent drop in
body temperature when
you get out will help to
induce sleep. Making
sure your bedroom is well
ventilated, by leaving a
window partially open, if
possible, can also help.

Start writing your own story

Say "no" more

Society can lead us to believe that we always
have to make ourselves available. If we turn down
someone's request for help, we fear we will be
viewed as lazy or, worse, uncaring. But what if
saying "yes" all the time is compromising your own
mental health? Taking on more and more tasks
and projects can see your stress levels soar, as you
attempt to juggle additional life admin. Next time
someone asks you for a favour that involves giving
up your precious time, stop and consider whether
it's something you can really take on, before
agreeing. It's OK (and wise) to say "no" sometimes.

DON'T FEAR
SOLITUDE

When it comes to anxiety, the thought of being alone will evoke different emotions in different people. For some, the prospect of solitude will come as a welcome relief, especially when struggling with social anxiety, or feeling panicky in large crowds or public places. For others, time alone may bring with it a crushing loneliness – a not-so-peaceful quietness that may see anxious thoughts quickly spiralling out of control, and the voice inside your head getting louder and harder to ignore.

If your experience is more like the latter, time alone can be difficult. But instead of fearing it, try to embrace it; reframe loneliness as a calmer, more productive state: solitude. How might you make your time alone more meaningful? Could you pursue a creative endeavour, practise meditation or yoga, or partake in some self-care? Filling your time with an enjoyable, fulfilling activity will help to ease the anxiety you might otherwise feel while alone, as well as nurturing and nourishing your well-being.

SLOW
DOWN

When we think about anxiety, we often picture a racing mind, a roller coaster of disordered thoughts and the stress that comes with a fast-paced, modern life. Sometimes, one of the easiest ways to combat this kind of anxiety is to slow down.

Taking a conscious step back from the frenetic pace at which we live can seem scary at first, but actively pressing the pause button is an important act of self-care. Often, a few small adjustments are enough to help us feel more grounded, calm and peaceful. Simple steps include: always taking your full lunch break, rather than working through it while eating a sandwich at your desk; leaving or stopping work on time each evening; rescheduling that night out when all you really feel like doing is curling up with a good book; and aiming to go to bed half an hour earlier than usual. These changes could all make the world of difference to how you feel, in both your body and mind. Slow is good for the soul.

KNOW WHEN
(AND WHERE)
TO SEEK SUPPORT

If you've tried many of the self-help suggestions offered within these pages, but don't feel they are easing your anxiety, it might be a good idea to seek the help and support of someone you trust, or consult a professional, in order to give yourself the best chance of recovery.

If seeking support online, be mindful of the information you're accessing. Choose trusted, reputable sites only, such as registered charities, and be aware that responsible websites will always contain trigger warnings to keep you safe, if you're feeling vulnerable.

Mindfulness, meditation and yoga apps can be a great way of making self-care a daily habit, which will go a long way to promoting good mental health.

Of course, getting advice that's personalized is sometimes the best way to go, so if you don't feel you're getting value from other sources, it's important to make an appointment with your doctor, who will listen to your symptoms and be able to offer confidential advice.

There are so many places you can go to access support, so don't feel you have to suffer in silence: you deserve happiness.

Reach out to others

If you've kept quiet about your anxiety, opening up to even just one person – a close friend or family member – can feel like a release. There are no hard-and-fast rules when it comes to speaking out about your own mental health, so take your time and be prepared for questions. You will likely find your loved one will be concerned, supportive and caring, but they may also be surprised, or even sad, as learning of someone else's struggles can sometimes be hard to hear. Remember that their reaction is no reflection on you: you're doing a brave thing by being honest about your feelings.

YOU'VE SURVIVED EVERY BAD EXPERIENCE YOU'VE EVER ENCOUNTERED

WHAT
ABOUT
CBT?

Cognitive behavioural therapy (CBT) is a form of talking therapy designed to help you understand and change your thinking patterns. By helping you realize the interconnected nature of your thoughts, feelings, emotions and behaviours, CBT can help you notice the vicious cycle you are stuck in, before supporting you to take the necessary steps in creating change.

Numerous studies point toward the effectiveness of CBT as a means of treating common mental health problems, including anxiety, and it's also endorsed by the National Institute for Health and Care Excellence (NICE) in the UK and the National Institutes of Health (NIH) in the USA.

Rather than a therapist giving you all the answers, CBT is very much a collaborative process. It usually involves a series of sessions with a qualified professional, at the end of which you'll have developed your own set of coping strategies.

Asking for help isn't
a sign of weakness,
it's a sign of strength.

Barack Obama

Counselling:
what to expect

While counselling is often
an umbrella term used to
describe a range of talking
therapies, it's also a therapy
in its own right. During a
session, a counsellor will
listen non-judgementally
as you open up about your
feelings, thoughts and emotions.
Unlike some other therapists, a
counsellor will not offer advice
– many people find having the
space to air their worries
beneficial, as being able to
talk freely can give you
the clarity you need to
find your own solutions.

ALTERNATIVE
THERAPIES

As well as more conventional talking therapies, many people also turn to alternative therapies when it comes to treating and managing anxiety. There are a range of options out there, so it's worth doing a little research and, if something makes sense to you, investigating further.

Examples of alternative therapies include hypno-therapy, which may be useful in stopping repetitive negative thought-patterns, and aromatherapy, which uses essential oils to help rebalance both body and mind.

Reiki – commonly referred to as energy healing – is another alternative therapy, in which a practitioner is said to transfer universal energy from their palms to your body, in order to promote healing and aid relaxation.

The proponents of these practices are convinced of the benefits and, while their effectiveness is hard to prove in scientific terms, all are said to have a calming effect, which can ease both the mental and physical symptoms of anxiety.

Online support forums

Sometimes it's easiest to open up to people who understand how you're feeling, which is why online support forums can help. Being able to chat openly with others who know what anxiety feels like, while remaining anonymous, can give you the freedom to express your innermost thoughts to a network of people who won't judge you, and who truly get it. Make sure the forum is reputable – for example, run in connection with a mental health charity – and that it's moderated responsibly.

Choosing a therapist

If you decide to seek professional support for your anxiety, choosing a therapist you are happy with is key. Before committing to booking lots of sessions or parting with any money, always make sure the therapist is fully qualified and registered with a professional body. If possible, have a conversation with them beforehand – are they someone you feel you could build a rapport with? Feeling comfortable with them and confident in their ability will help you to get the most out of your sessions together.

BE PATIENT
WITH YOURSELF

Anxiety, worry and stress can be all-encompassing, and sometimes when you're caught in the midst of it, it's easy to forget that this is not who you are. Even a short struggle can feel like a lifetime when you're lost inside your mind; so if you've been battling with anxiety for years, it's normal to have begun fully identifying with these thoughts, feelings and emotions. Perhaps you've even started defining yourself as "an anxious person".

But it won't always have been this way – and by applying a little conscious awareness to the anxious states you experience, you can move beyond it once more. Always hold onto the truth that you will feel happy, free and peaceful again. And until then, be patient with yourself.

This
too shall
pass

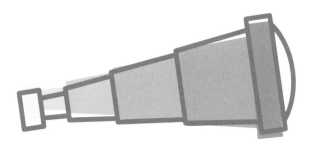

If you knew you could
handle anything that
came your way, what would
you possibly have to fear?
The answer is: nothing!

Susan Jeffers

Conclusion

Hopefully, the information and advice within these pages has helped you to feel a little less alone, as well as better equipped to address any worry or anxiety that you may face, both now and in the future. As well as learning how important self-care is in controlling your stress levels, one of the keys to anxiety management is the understanding that you can choose to change your mindset in the face of adversity, even if the adverse situation cannot be immediately resolved.

Remember that you can always turn to professional support if you need it, but the important thing is to go gently – changing your mindset won't always happen overnight, so be patient and kind to yourself. After all, you've shown great bravery by making the decision to take these first steps... and this is just the beginning of your journey. You've got this!

Resources

For further help and information, you may find the following useful:

Anxiety UK
This charity provides information, support and understanding for those living with anxiety disorders. **anxietyuk.org.uk**

Beat
This charity helps to guide and support those suffering from eating disorders, as well as their loved ones. **beateatingdisorders.org.uk**

CALM
The Campaign Against Living Miserably is leading a movement against suicide. **thecalmzone.net**

Mind
This charity offers support and advice to help empower anyone experiencing a mental health problem. **mind.org.uk**

Samaritans
A 24-hour, free, confidential helpline to support anyone, whatever they might be going through.
samaritans.org; 116 123; jo@samaritans.org

FOR READERS IN THE USA
Anxiety & Depression Association of America (ADAA)
Education, training and research for anxiety, depression and related disorders. **adaa.org**

Mental Health America (MHA)
Promoting the overall mental health of all Americans. **mhanational.org**

Image credits

If you're interested in finding out more about our books, find us on Facebook at SUMMERSDALE PUBLISHERS and follow us on Twitter at @SUMMERSDALE.

WWW.SUMMERSDALE.COM